# What happens when people die?

# What is on the other side?

Now you can know what lies on the other side of death.

Whether you face the loss of a loved one or are merely curious about death and the life after, this powerful little book offers a message of insight, comfort and hope.

**Death and the Life After** will help you regard the mystique of death with a new courage, with greater confidence in an afterlife more magnificent than anything eye has seen or ear has heard.

IAN BARCLAY

# Death and the Life After

First Printing, January 1992


Published by
HERE'S LIFE PUBLISHERS, INC.
P. O. Box 1576
San Bernardino, CA 92402

Cover design by Garborg Design Works
Interior design by Barbara Sherrill


**Library of Congress Cataloging-in-Publication Data**
Barclay, Ian.
    Death and the life after : what happens when people die? :
what is on the other side? / Ian Barclay.
        p.        cm.
    ISBN 0-89840-346-4
    1. Death—Religious aspects—Christianity. 2. Future life—
Christianity. I. Title.
BT825.B29        1992
236'.1—dc20                        91-36765
                                        CIP

Unless indicated otherwise, Scripture quotations are from *The Holy Bible: New International Version,* © 1973, 1978, 1984 by the International Bible Society. Published by Zondervan Bible Publishers, Grand Rapids, Michigan.

Scripture quotations designated NAS are from *The New American Standard Bible,* © The Lockman Foundation 1960, 1962, 1963, 1968, 1971, 1972, 1975, 1977.

**For More Information, Write:**
*L.I.F.E.*—P.O. Box A399, Sydney South 2000, Australia
*Campus Crusade for Christ of Canada*—Box 300, Vancouver, B.C., V6C 2X3, Canada
*Campus Crusade for Christ*—Pearl Assurance House, 4 Temple Row, Birmingham, B2 5HG, England
*Lay Institute for Evangelism*—P.O. Box 8786, Auckland 3, New Zealand
*Campus Crusade for Christ*—P.O. Box 240, Raffles City Post Office, Singapore 9117
*Great Commission Movement of Nigeria*—P.O. Box 500, Jos, Plateau State Nigeria, West Africa
*Campus Crusade for Christ International*—100 Sunport Lane, Orlando, FL 32809, U.S.A.

# Contents

# The
# Way Out

# Introduction

In the film *Chariots of Fire*, Eric Liddell is the central figure, but the story also touches on the life of Harold Abrahams, a Cambridge athletics blue and Olympic gold medalist. While Eric Liddell became a missionary in the Far East, Harold Abrahams joined the British Broadcasting Corporation.

The trouble Harold Abrahams took in preparing for a broadcast became legendary. Brian Johnston once illustrated Abrahams' meticulous attention to detail by referring to a little booklet he had produced. Johnston writes, "It was typical of [Abrahams'] love of detail and must have involved much journeying to and fro on the Underground [London's subway system]. The booklet showed where all the 'Way Out' signs were situated on every London station, and the number of the train which always stopped exactly opposite the exit."

One word the Bible uses for death is *exodus,* which means "the way out." In this book, I want to look at the emotional, biblical, physical and Christian experience of death, so that when a member of our family or a friend dies, we will know what is happening to them and to us. I also hope it will be used to give away to friends and neighbors when they ask about death and the life after.

It would be hard to attempt to write a book like this without some experience of the matter. My first wife died after battling with cancer for nine years. As an Anglican clergyman, I had often tried to help other people in their loss and had performed hundreds of funeral services, but it wasn't until Sheila's death that I understood something of the trauma involved. Those who suffer this way are called "bereaved," coming from the word *reave,* meaning "to ravage, rob and leave desolate."

It is out of this experience that I write. I want to try to make bereavement understandable and bearable for those who go through it, as well as providing a helpful summary of the basic Christian teaching on death and the life to come.

Ian Barclay

# 1

# Sorrow Comes to Everybody

# The Emotional Experience
## of Death

Grief and *sorrow* are nearly always the first aspects of death to touch us. Although it is possible to live to middle age without having to face death in our family or circle of friends, eventually it will happen and we will be confronted with the perplexing experience of bereavement.

In America, close to three million people die every year. Inevitably, we will be part of those figures one day, and before that time they must include members of our family and some of our close friends.

We need to prepare ourselves by trying to understand the subject as fully as possible, always keeping in mind the final limitation that complete knowledge can't be ours until we experience the event.

# A Grief Observed

Grief is an emotional wound with several recognizable symptoms. Colin Parkes describes it this way: "When a love-tie is severed, an emotional and behavioral reaction is set in [motion] which we call grief." He goes on to say, "Newly bereaved people are often surprised and frightened by the sheer intensity of their sorrows."

Every experience of grief is deeply personal and highly individual. It would be impossible to list the symptoms we will feel or to place them in the order in which they will come. No two experiences of grief are the same because the people and circumstances involved are always different. However, if you stop to map out a time of grief after it has happened, there are patterns of behavior and emotions that are similar.

## Tears

Crying is a mechanism which the body uses to release tension. If we are a

typical male, we may have tried to sup-
press tears with a stiff upper lip. In the
ordinary events of life, tears can also be
suppressed by deliberately choosing
laughter to ease tension.

In everyday experiences, the emotional adjustments are small, but in bereavement they can be of mountainous
proportions. At such times the body will
often choose tears as an emergency
safety valve. During these times, crying
can be as uncontrollable as it is un-
wanted.

Jim Graham, the pastor of Goldhill
Baptist Church, tells how he received
news in Singapore of his father's death—
a death which, because of recent ill
health, was not entirely unexpected. The
Grahams were leaving for the Philippines
the next morning and so decided to go
out for a meal with friends as planned.

Jim Graham continues, "I had just
closed the door behind us as we made
our way to the restaurant for our meal,
when I was suddenly, unexpectedly and
publicly overwhelmed with tears. They
shook me quite uncontrollably—and I
felt so foolish and terribly embarrassed
and exposed."

Jim's experience is typical of what can happen at a time of bereavement.

## Anger

Elizabeth Heike, a committed Christian, tells how, after the death of a friend who had had a terminal illness, she was angry with God.

"It had taken me a long time to face the fact that I was angry at all," she says, "but to be angry with Him who had shown me so much of His love during Madeline's illness and after her death seemed ungrateful and a denial of the reality of that experience."

Bereaved Christians who feel guilty about their anger need to take this to heart: Jesus was also angry about death. At the grave of Lazarus we are told He was "deeply moved in his spirit and troubled." Another version says, "He gave way to such distress of spirit as made his body tremble." The words imply not only that He experienced grief, but also intense anger at the unnaturalness of death.

Death wasn't part of God's original plan. It came as a direct result of man's sin. Jesus seems repelled at the whole idea of the death of a very dear friend.

We mustn't be surprised if someone, in the confusion of grief, says, "Why has God allowed this to happen to me?" The Bible is clear in its answer. It is the sinfulness of man which has brought death into the world. Only confused and distraught thinking lays the responsibility for it at God's door. God is the One who offers eternal life through His Son.

Still, anger remains part of grief and it can be vented on God, the minister, the family or a friend. We must be understanding when we see it.

## Shock and Numbness

When told that her husband had been killed in an accident at work, one woman fainted. When she came to, she wanted to know what had happened. When told, she fainted again. In all, she fainted five times before she could receive the information without reacting violently.

Some people can be literally struck dumb with grief. Others are just numb, unable to take in what has happened.

Until they do, they live in a dazed and dream-like state, unable to think clearly.

## Fantasy

Fantasy happens at two very different levels. On one level, some people "see" their lost loved one in a crowd for days, perhaps even weeks, after the death. It is as though the brain is scanning for a familiar image but once the crowd comes into sharp focus the fantasy disappears.

At another level, the fantasy becomes a rejection of reality. At this point, there is the irrational belief that the death hasn't happened. A place will be set at the dining-room table or a room will constantly be prepared for the loved one's return.

In all experiences of grief, gentle and comforting counsel is essential. Where there is a loss of reality, professional help must be sought.

## Guilt

As an Anglican minister, I can't remember counseling anyone going through grief without finding that guilt was also involved. I've often heard a wife

say, "If only we had taken that last vaca-
tion together," or a grown man lament,
"If only I had been a more considerate
son."

Guilt is the most natural reaction
when we lose someone we love. We must
expect it and recognize it when it comes.
The human condition and the failure it
brings mean that we can never be the
people we would like to be. When someone is alive, we can pretend that we are
better than we are. In a very stark way,
death can obliterate the memory of the
joys we may have given in a relationship,
and we remember only the failures and
shortcomings.

If, after reflection, we are still aware
of failure, we must confess it and roll our
burden, as Peter suggests, on to the
shoulders of our God who is able to bear
it in a way that our human frame can't
(1 Peter 5:7).

## Exhaustion

There will be tiredness. A bereaved
person referring to the "feeling of being
utterly drained and exhausted" went on
to say, "This is hardly surprising because grief is work and most of our ener-

gy will be required to do it. Deep in our minds and spirits, emotions and thoughts must be encountered, experienced and worked through."

Someone else said that the sheer tiredness of grief didn't begin to lift until she had had more than a year of relaxed, normal sleep.

## How Long Will Grief Last?

The important thing is not to anticipate the length of time, but to recognize that we must deal with grief at our own pace. It can't be measured against someone else's timetable. There will be tides that ebb and flow, but we are probably talking about a year for the first step on the road to recovery. Some people find anniversaries, birthdays or holidays extremely difficult to cope with. They can be traumatic for many years.

## The Need to Talk

"Give sorrow words" is an important piece of advice. In *The Lament*, Anton Chekhov tells the story of Iona Potapov whose son had died. No one seemed willing to listen to him, so to find relief he finally poured out the whole sad story to his horse. The story is powerful because it is so real. Part of the healing process of grief is being able to talk about the feelings. Not to do so may hinder the healing process from even beginning.

There are those exceptional cases where people just need someone to sit with them. Beethoven wasn't a man known for his social graces. His deafness meant that conversation was often difficult. When he heard of the death of a friend's son, he hurried over to the house to give comfort. Finding a piano in the room, he sat down and played for half an hour, pouring out his love and concern through the music. When he had finished, he left without saying a word. Later the friend said that no other visit had been so beneficial.

Whether the reaction is crying, the need to talk, anger or fear, it must come out and be dealt with in a natural way. Any suppressed or repressed feelings will ultimately cause problems until they are dealt with.

## The Scriptures Saved My Life

Oliver Cromwell was plunged into utter despair and misery when his son

Robert died at the early age of seventeen. Twenty years later he said that Philippians 4:13 ("I can do everything through Him who gives me strength") "once saved me when my eldest son died, which went as a dagger to my heart."

Bereavement strikes like a dagger and many have found comfort in the Bible. There is one relationship that transcends death and that is the one we can have with God, which is fed and strengthened by the Bible. The calming words of the Psalms or the words of Jesus to His disciples nourish the soul, and bereavement is a time when the soul can feel particularly dry.

## Learning to Live Again

As with all wounds, grief eventually heals. For some, the process takes a long while, but time is a good medicine and normal life will eventually return. Like any deep wound, there will be a scar which will never disappear. It wouldn't be right if loved ones were completely forgotten. How could they be?

Gradually, when the trauma has passed and the threads of life are taken up again, the wonderful creativity of our

God is such that He can bring a new wholeness into our lives, even new relationships. That is my own experience.

When Sheila died, I suppose like any man in his late forties, I felt that I would have to settle down to life alone. In a very short time I met Hazel. At first, I was frightened of being disloyal to my previous marriage by appearing to believe that someone could easily take Sheila's place. Then I realized that could never happen. What I was being offered was a completely new relationship, and in no way was it to be compared with the first.

I will never forget Sheila, but I now am in awe at the creativity of God, who can restore life by giving someone new to love, which, after all, is a very basic human need.

# 2

# Death
# Is a
# Thoroughfare

# The Words Used in the Bible to Describe Death

It may sound rather depressing to open a Bible and trace the meaning of words such as *death* and *dying,* but the reverse is true. Not only is it revealing, but it is also quite fascinating to see the writers struggle within the limitations of human language to describe something that will take them and us beyond the grave.

## Death Is a Thoroughfare

There are one or two words in the New Testament that have a twentieth-century ring to them and suggest that man's life can come to an abrupt end. But these are very rare. The most frequently used words speak of the physical, material part of man, that is his body, being separated from the spiritual part, his soul. The thrust of the New Testament is, as Victor Hugo put it, "Death is a thoroughfare, not a blind alley."

It isn't that some people go down the road of death and emerge in heaven while others get no further than the grave. Death is a thoroughfare down which all men and women make their way. Some will do it unwillingly, but the same life-force that brought us into this world will propel us into the next.

This must be the thought in the apostle Peter's mind when he speaks about his "departure" (2 Peter 1:15). The Greek word is *exodus*, which as well as being the title for the second book of the Bible is also a description of its contents, namely the exit or exodus of the Hebrew people from the land of Egypt. In the most basic terms, the story of the exodus is the history of people moving from one place to another.

## Eternity in the Minds of Men

Most civilizations and cultures have a strong belief in life after death. The Bible teaches us to expect this. Solomon says that God "has also set eternity in the hearts of men" (Ecclesiastes 3:11). In the creation story we are told that "God breathed *lives* into man" (a literal translation of Genesis 2:7). The word for *life* in the original is in the plural. Eternity is not only put within man's intellectual grasp, but he also has an in-built mechanism preparing him for the experience.

When we look back into history, we find that ancient man was certainly aware of eternity. One of the earliest books available is called *The Book of the Dead,* a collection of prayers and formulae whereby the dead might communicate and find their way about. It is interesting that the oldest known name for a coffin, again coming from ancient Egypt, is "a chest of the living."

## Beyond the Exit

Although it cannot be taken as an exact parallel, Exodus can be used as a picture of all that happens to us when we leave this world. The people of Israel, having made their exodus from Egypt, found two areas before them: the wilderness and the promised land. For them, these two experiences were consecutive.

They had to pass through one to enjoy the other. For every person who leaves this world, there are two similar areas before them—but they are not experienced consecutively. As we go down the thoroughfare called death, we will see either the scenery of the wilderness or the promised land. It will be one or the other, but not both.

# The Wilderness

The Bible uses two main words to describe the experience we summarize in English as "hell." Both have the idea of a wilderness. The first, found in the Old Testament, is the Hebrew word *Sheol*—the place of the departed. *Sheol* is the grey pit, a shadowy place, where men move about in ghostly form in an environment entirely devoid of color and joy.

The main New Testament word translated "hell" is *Gehenna*. This word paints the frightening picture of Ge Hinnom, Jerusalem's large rubbish dump and public incinerator tucked away from sight in the Valley of Hinnom. Ge Hinnom was a desolate place that perpetually smoldered, where the rubbish and the heat caused a particularly unpleasant species of worm to live and breed rapidly.

Both the pit of Sheol and the Valley of Hinnom suggest places that are hidden away, silent and colorless in the depths of the earth from which there is no escape. This would seem to be confirmed by our Anglo-Saxon word *hell*, which comes from the verb *hele*, meaning "to hide." This word is still used by gardeners today when they speak of "heeling in" the roots of a plant as they cover them with earth.

Those who arrive in hell will not be able to escape and will certainly be conscious of the awfulness of their surroundings. Jesus makes this quite clear in the story of the rich man and Lazarus. The rich man in hell sees, speaks and feels regret as he recalls the past. This point is emphasized by the number of times Jesus says there will be "wailing and gnashing of teeth."

# An Awfully Big Adventure

Before we begin to look at heaven, we must first consider death from a Christian point of view. Victor Hugo's statement about the thoroughfare fails to give the sense of release, purpose and excitement that is always part of the New Testament word for death. In fact, after reading the New Testament, you almost find yourself saying with James Barrie's Peter Pan, "To die will be an awfully big adventure."

Like the apostle Peter, Paul also speaks of the fact that the time for his "departure" has come (2 Timothy 4:6). However, Paul uses the word *analusis*. This word conjures up three vivid pictures of death for the Christian.

*Analusis* is a word which was used for the freeing of a slave. As the slave departs to freedom, you would hardly expect him to regard the event with morbid introspection. His mind, gripped by the experience of release, would race on to begin savoring the broad expanses of liberty. John Fletcher of Madeley understood this when he wrote: "What is it to die but to open our eyes after the disagreeable dream of life. It is to break the prison of corrupt flesh and blood."

In this century, we see an example of the eagerness for the liberty death brings in the last postcard of Dr. F. B. Meyer.

While lying ill at Boscombe, he addressed a postcard to Mr. A. Lindsay Glegg with a very shaky hand. He wrote, "I have raced you to heaven. I am just off—see you there. Love, F. B. Meyer."

How different this is from the attitude of those outside the Christian faith. As he lay dying on June 5, 1910, the American short story writer O. Henry called to the nurse for a candle. When she asked why he wanted it, he replied, "Because I am afraid to go home in the dark."

This word *departure* (*analusis*) was also used by the philosophers for a problem that had been resolved. It meant the problem had gone and the answer had come. Intellectual light shone where there had been darkness. That is why Professor C. E. M. Joad once said that he was looking forward to death because it would bring the answer to many of the perplexing things that had puzzled him.

Christians of every age have regarded death in this way. "Now for the morning and the King's face. No more night and no more darkness," was the passionate cry of Donald Cargill just before he was martyred in Edinburgh in 1681.

The most interesting use of *analusis* is connected with ships. It is the word for the last rope to be cast off, thus freeing a ship to begin its journey. The vessel, having been held to the dock, is now free and her bow swings out toward the harbor mouth.

Lord Tennyson used this figure of death in his poem, "Crossing the Bar." The journey is not past but about to begin. The whole atmosphere of the word speaks of the excitement of adventure.

Above all, we must not forget that death is not a new route. Michael Green makes this point when he speaks of Vasco da Gama, the great Portuguese sailor, who was the first to circumnavigate the southernmost tip of Africa. As Vasco da Gama sailed around the Cape, he changed its name from the "Cape of Storms" to the "Cape of Good Hope." As Christians, we take heart from the fact that Jesus has already died and has risen again. Death has been circumnavigated.

# Traveler, What Lies Over the Hill?

As we turn to look at heaven, we may echo George MacDonald's question, "Traveler, what lies over the hill?"

Reinhold Niebuhr said, "It is unwise for Christians to claim any knowledge of either the furniture of heaven or of the temperature of hell." Yet when we look at what Jesus says, we find an amazing wealth of detail.

It would be wrong to interpret the phrase, "In my Father's house are many rooms" (John 14:2), to mean western-style housing with twentieth-century rooms. Dr. Westcott begins to lead us back to the picture Jesus must have had in mind when he tells us that the word *rooms* had the meaning of a resting place or a station on a great road where travelers found refreshment.

Archbishop Temple tells us that the word means a wayside caravanserai. A caravanserai was the motel for the camel caravans which crossed the great areas of the ancient world. A caravanserai probably consisted of a single building where the proprietor and his family lived. The main feature would have been space to park with a watering place for the animals and somewhere to pitch a tent. If the caravanserai was in a desert, then it would have the atmosphere of an oasis, complete with trees providing shade from the relentless glare of the sun. At night, when all the guests had arrived and the animals were secured, a friendly, convivial spirit prevailed.

## No Admission Except on Business

When Florence Nightingale was told that a loved one had died and gone "to be at rest," she replied, "Oh, no! I am sure the next life is immense activity." That is the view of the New Testament, though our hymnbooks often give us the idea of inactivity and boring repetition. Even in Heber's glorious hymn, *Holy, Holy, Holy,* we seem to be condemned to endlessly "casting down our golden crowns beside a glassy sea."

The New Testament view is that after death comes paradise, a fertile garden where the caravan comes to rest in the middle of a desert. It is a place where men and women are engaged in all the activities of recreation.

## Your Reservation

A caravan's progress across the desert was constantly hindered by slipping loads and escaping children. Therefore, the prospect of the caravanserai would be even more eagerly awaited by the weary travelers. However, the vision of welcome and refreshment may well have been dulled by the depressing anxiety that the lateness of the arrival might mean a "No Vacancy" sign at the end of a hard day's journey.

To ensure that this didn't happen, early in the day the caravan master would send his servant ahead to secure the appropriate reservation. This process of guaranteeing a secure place is also part of the teaching of Jesus. He tells His disciples that He has gone ahead to prepare a place for them (John 14:2).

## All Roads Do Not Lead to Heaven

With so much detail, it is surprising that the disciples wanted still more information. Perhaps only a doubter like Thomas could ask the necessary question and point to the one apparent flaw in all that Jesus had said. You can almost hear Thomas saying, "We are glad that heaven is like a caravanserai and as real as a place on a map. We are delighted that our reservations are secure as if someone has personally gone ahead to book them. But how can we find the way to this heavenly resting place? There are neither roads nor signposts in a desert, much less on the way to heaven."

Jesus replies, "I am the way and the truth and the life. No one comes to the Father except through Me" (John 14:6).

This remark refutes the illogical thought that all roads lead to heaven. Roads, after all, go in two directions—both to and from the place we have in mind. So, once we have chosen the right road we must also choose the right direction.

Jesus said that He is "the way," that is, the right road. He went on to say that He is "the truth," the right direction along the right road. He then added that He is "the life," suggesting that He can give us the power to take us down the right road in the right direction. We can hardly ask for more than that.

## Nothing Profane Shall Enter In

Toward the end of the Bible we find a forceful reminder that must be included in any teaching on heaven. John tells us that nothing unclean will enter God's final kingdom (Revelation 21:27).

Christianity is an ethical religion. It lays down a standard and teaches that one day we will be measured against it. Each action and every word uttered will be measured against the divine yardstick. We may excuse ourselves for each failure and kind heaven may be forgiving, but even a cursory inward glance will tell us that we have fallen short of God's standard. As Isaiah says with a quiet wit and wisdom, "All our righteous acts are like filthy rags" (Isaiah 64:6).

The heart of the gospel is that in dying on the cross for our sins, Jesus became our "righteousness" (2 Corinthians 5:21) so that we might be allowed into heaven. Paul says, "If anyone is in Christ, he is a new creation" (2 Corinthians 5:17). Heaven is populated by those who have been made new by Jesus. For the Christian, judgment is therefore past and entrance to heaven is secured.

# The Last Judgment

In his revelation, the apostle John speaks of a "great white throne" (Revelation 20:11), where the final judgment of sinners will take place. The followers of Christ will escape this, although they will have to stand before a "judgment seat" (Romans 14:10), something quite separate and different. The word is *bema,* and it describes the place where the judge stood at the ancient athletic games to watch the athletes compete and from where he would present rewards and prizes at the conclusion of the event.

Every Christian will one day stand before the *bema* of Christ. Their entrance into heaven is beyond doubt, but they will be rewarded according to how they have lived as Christians (see 1 Corinthians 3:12-15).

# 3

# The
# Supreme
# Festival

# The Physical Experience

Dietrich Bonhoeffer, the German pastor executed by the Nazis on the day before World War II ended, called death "the supreme festival on the road to freedom." We will now look at the physical phenomena of death, and perhaps discover why Bonhoeffer regarded the day of his death like this.

## The Body Stops Working

In physical terms, death takes place when the handful of chemicals which make up the physical apparatus of the human body cease to work. It is nothing less than a miracle that God has managed to breathe life into such a meager handful of ordinary elements. If you take a wheelbarrow to your local chemist, you will need three pounds of calcium, twelve ounces of potassium, eight ounces of sulphur, two pounds of phosphorus, thirty-six pounds of charcoal and a trace of sodium. On the way home, drop by the hardware store and buy a medium-size nail and then add 140 pounds of water. You now have all the component chemicals that make up a human being. Only the miracle of life is lacking.

It is easy to see why many people with little or no spiritual insight place such importance on the body. It is "them," all they have. Consequently, they do everything they can to protect and cultivate their bodies. However, the Christian's attitude should have a different emphasis.

## Man Wears God's Image

God said, "Let us make man wearing our own image and likeness." This Knox translation of Genesis 1:26 emphasizes, as the Hebrew does, that the word *image* refers to the fact that God has shared His outward appearance with us. This immediately lifts us above the rest of the created world.

There are also inward characteristics which God has shared with man. We have the power of thought, of feeling and of will. We are also like Him in that we are self-conscious and, to some degree, self-determining. In the beginning, man even shared a moral likeness with God because he was created good. But because of the fall, when Adam and Eve chose to disobey God, man is scarred and marred by sin like the rest of creation.

In spite of this, the Christian would still want to say that man is so much more than Desmond Morris' "vertical, hunting, weapon-toting, territorial, neotenous, brainy, Naked Ape, a primate by ancestry and a carnivore by adoption."

## Man Is Spirit

Having accomplished the redemption of the human race on the cross, Jesus cried out, "Father, into Your hands I commit My spirit." Notice that Jesus didn't say "myself" or "my body," but "my spirit." The spirit is the other side of man's nature and the side which needs to be "born again." If a developing relationship with God is to be encouraged, it is the spirit of man that needs to be nourished by worship and fed with the "meat" of the Scriptures.

# What Actually Happens When We Die?

When the body ceases to function, *I* don't stop being *me*. When I die, I leave this portable piece of plumbing behind and it either decomposes in the grave or is returned to dust and ashes by fire. But the spirit lives on, and departs for its spiritual, eternal destination. Jesus said to the penitent thief, "Today you will be with Me in paradise."

Socrates uttered a profound truth on his death bed when he said, "Bury me if you can catch me." All that can be caught is the empty container that had once held a human being.

It is undeniable that the human body can be very attractive. When we are inhabiting them as stewards, we have a responsibility to honor them, remembering always in whose image we are made. There are few things, if any, more valuable than a human body when indwelt by a human being. But it is sentimentalism to carry this beyond the grave.

## A Clinical Definition of Death

Doctors are still debating an exact medical definition of death, so a layman like myself is unlikely to come up with a definitive answer. For thousands of years, death has been recognized by the failure of certain parts of the body. Until twenty years ago, a man or woman who had no pulse and who had ceased to breathe was said to be dead.

Today, various machines can deal with these failures, hence the concept of "brain death." This is when the brain stem has ceased to function and artificial support to the other parts of the body becomes pointless. So a clinical definition of death now must include a recognition of brain death and not simply the failure of heart, lungs and kidneys, as in previous years.

## The Fear of Death

The Victorians had a morbid fascination with death, but they hardly ever spoke about sex. Our generation appears to have reversed these subjects. However, the fear of death is universal.

The Duke of Wellington said that "a man must be a coward or a liar who could boast of never having felt a fear of death." Fear of death is inevitable because, apart from Lazarus and a few other biblical characters, no human being has been through the complete process of death and come back again.

Christians, however, do have the assurance that Jesus has "destroyed death." In the New Testament the word is *katargeo* and it literally means, "rendered ineffective." We still have to face death and we may worry about the way it will come to us, but because Jesus has made it ineffectual, death won't be able to hold us. That is the point.

## Out-of-Body Experiences

The last few years have seen an increasing recognition of "out-of-body experiences," often referred to simply as OBEs. People who have had serious accidents and been revived, or patients who have "died" for a few moments on the operating table while undergoing critical surgery, claim on recovery that they have had a glimpse of the afterlife.

In the 1970s, a group of doctors arose who called themselves "thanatologists" or those who "study what happens after death." Dr. Raymond Moody wrote an international bestseller titled *Life After Life*, in which he detailed hundreds of OBEs. Dr. Moody claims that his research neither proves nor disproves that there is life after death or that heaven and hell exist.

Other writers on the subject are not so cautious. Dr. Maurice Rawlings claims that OBEs prove the reality of Christianity, although some of the patients involved who have been resuscitated would repudiate this.

In *The Lion Book of Beliefs*, John Allan makes an important point in his section titled "Mysteries," when he says, "Thanatological experiences 'prove' very little. They afford grounds for fascinating speculation, but no more." He concludes that "it is hard to tell the exact moment at which someone passes from life to death" and therefore an OBE might be "a fantasy conjured up by some region of the patient's brain."

The tabloids continually run stories of those who claim to have died and come back from the dead. When these are brought to our attention, we must insist that there is no evidence for the reality of these claims, and they certainly don't add anything to all that the Scriptures have taught. The Bible must be the source of our doctrines and beliefs, rather than the writings of the sensation-seeking press.

## The End Is the Beginning

Before he was executed on April 8, 1945, Dietrich Bonhoeffer sent this message to George Bell, Bishop of Chichester: "This is the end—but for me it is the beginning." That is how Christians should look at death.

Wing-Commander Branse Burbridge was highly decorated for his night fighter missions over Germany during World War II. His story was recorded in the bestseller, *Night Fighter,* by Rawnsley and Wright.

Burbridge and Skelton, the two-man mosquito crew, established a record number of enemy aircraft shot down by a night fighter. On every flight over Ger-

many, and especially when engaging
enemy aircraft in combat, they took
death into their own hands. This is how
Branse Burbridge describes his first dog-
fight:

> In our first real scrap, our op-
> ponent seemed to be out-turning me; I
> turned tighter than ever and banked
> very steeply—this "toppled" the instru-
> ments, which would take twenty
> minutes to reset themselves. So even if
> he didn't get us first, we might spin into
> the sea . . . I felt prickly—I was afraid.
> Then something hit me, but it wasn't a
> bullet! In a split second, I realized two
> things; both stemmed from the fact that
> I was a Christian.
>
> First, if God had further work for
> me to do for Him after the war, I was
> bound to survive; second, if I did get
> killed, death would be literally the
> gateway to heaven, and I should see the
> Lord Jesus Christ. So what did it mat-
> ter?
>
> The new life that Jesus Christ had
> given me is eternal, and so I need not
> be afraid of death. In fact, I have not
> been afraid since then. But it took that
> dog-fight at night over Germany to
> make me see this.

When I leave this earth I shall live eternal life in Christ's presence. While I'm here I live it "at a distance." Through it, He has taught me so many lessons, guided me through so many problems, given me so much satisfaction, spoken to me so often, that my belief in the living Christ could never be destroyed. Try telling a pilot at an overseas station that the Royal Air Force does not exist—and he'll tell you you're talking through your helmet!

## The Joy of Dying

Final illness at the end of a long and happy life can hold the promise of a welcome release for many people. There are many among the elderly who approach death without any sense of apprehension. Indeed John Venn, to quote one famous case, was so filled with joy at the prospect of heaven that he actually lived an extra two weeks.

## The Greatest Adventure of My Life

James Casson was a young doctor who died in 1980. I heard him speak one Sunday morning at St. Ebbes, Oxford, and he tells his story in a little book

called *The Greatest Adventure of My Life*.
He says:

> Dying makes life suddenly real.
> Watching my slow physical deteriora-
> tion reaffirmed my belief that there is
> something else within, which would sur-
> vive if only because my personality
> stayed the same in spite of the eroding
> bodily form in which it is confined . . .
> Strange to relate, however, my life as a
> practicing Christian was changed by
> the knowledge that I was dying almost
> more than if I had been a committed
> atheist.
>
> Suddenly all I had been told or
> read in the Bible made sense. My life-
> style didn't change very much but my
> attitude did. It was as if I suddenly
> started really to live, although the
> reverse was true and I was dying. A
> clear spring morning is most meaning-
> ful after weeks of dull, wet weather. The
> slow build up of dust on a car wind-
> shield goes unnoticed till I clean it with
> a few squirts of water and the wind-
> shield wipers. So life can only really be
> understood when it is contrasted with
> death.

An understanding of death ought to
sharpen our focus on life and make us

want to enjoy every second until the moment when God takes us into eternity.

4

Easter
and the
Eastered

# The Christian Experience

Easter is at the heart of Christianity with its teaching that Jesus rose from the dead. Take away this central truth and the whole of Christianity collapses into a myth. (I will come back to this point later in the chapter when I touch on the historical evidence for the resurrection.)

Jesus is spoken of as one "who has destroyed death and has brought life and immortality to light through the gospel" (2 Timothy 1:10). This makes the writers of the New Testament extremely bold when they come to write about the eternal life to be enjoyed by the Christian. Paul, for example, uses the past tense to speak of eternity, in spite of the fact that we are still encumbered with a

physical body which will one day have to
die. Death is, therefore, an event we can
approach without fear. It has lost its
sting and its power to hold us. One day,
clothed in resurrection bodies, we will
enter eternity to enjoy the presence of
God forever.

## The Dawning of a New Day

To trace the New Testament idea of
life after death involves returning to the
Old Testament with its assumption that
life continues beyond the grave: "Then
Abraham breathed his last and died at a
good old age, an old man and full of
years; and he was *gathered to his people*"
(Genesis 25:8). Abraham was a great
man of faith so you might expect him to
be "gathered to" God, but no—he is to be
united with those of his family who lived
before him in previous generations.

The Old Testament scholar, Alec
Motyer, commenting on the phrase
"gathered to his people," says, "The
description as it stands is a telling revelation of the reality which life after death
possessed for those ancient times. He
[Abraham] went to join the company of
those who had gone before." Jacob had

the same hope when he presumed that
Joseph was dead and said, "In mourning
will I go down to the grave to my son"
(Genesis 37:35).

# Sheol

*Sheol* in the Old Testament is a
place-name and doesn't have the sig-
nificance that words like *hell* or *heaven*
have in the New Testament. Sheol was
the place *everybody* went to when they
died. Murderers, thieves and adulterers
went there, but so did those who served
God well. Alec Motyer says that "while
opinions may well differ in the interpreta-
tion of what the Old Testament tells
about the *nature of life* in Sheol, there
can be no disputing its insistence of the
*fact* of life in Sheol."

Old Testament men and women
described difficult times as "the snares of
death," but death itself was never
thought of as the end. During his life,
David said to God, "You guide me with
Your counsel, and afterward You will
take me into glory" (Psalm 73:24). A
twentieth-century follower of Jesus
Christ would not have to change those
Old Testament words by one letter to

describe his own certain hope for eternity.

For the men and women of the Old Testament, Sheol was a place where spiritual and moral differences were preserved (e.g., Psalm 49). Those who had served God well could expect "glory" and His enemies could expect adversity.

Although the idea of adversity was not explicitly developed, there were occasional warnings of the dangers of entering the next world with sin unconfessed, unrepented and, therefore, unforgiven. "But man, despite his riches, does not endure; he is like the beasts that perish. This is the fate of those who trust in themselves" (Psalm 49:12,13).

# The Empty Tomb

The most important of all the New Testament miracles is the resurrection of Jesus. Many people who have doubts about it have never stopped to consider the evidence. There have been several thorough studies of the facts by skilled lawyers who have examined the evidence much as they would in a court of law. The most famous of these lawyers is Frank Morison, who wrote *Who Moved*

*the Stone?* Another is Sir Norman Anderson, formerly Professor of Oriental Laws
and Director of the Institute of Advanced
Legal Studies in the University of London, who wrote *The Evidence for the
Resurrection.*

We must be honest about the
evidence and admit that it can only bring
us to the place where we say, "There is a
very high degree of possibility that Jesus
rose from the dead." What brings the
final conviction of certainty for most
people is to meet the risen Jesus. This is
what it means to be a Christian, to experience the cleansing from sin that He
offers, and to begin the new life He
makes available to those who follow Him.
Let us look at a few of the details of the
resurrection.

## Jesus Spoke Openly About It

When Jesus first spoke to the Jews
in picture language about His being
raised up "in three days" (John 2:19),
they misunderstood Him and thought He
was referring to Herod's Temple. They
replied, "It has taken forty-six years to
build this temple, and You are going to
raise it in three days?" It was only after

the resurrection had taken place that the disciples recalled what He had said (John 2:22).

From the moment Peter made his great confession of faith at Caesarea Philippi, "You are the Christ, the Son of the living God" (Matthew 16:16), Jesus began to explain to His disciples about the things which would take place in Jerusalem: how He would suffer at the hands of the elders and chief priests and be put to death, but "on the third day be raised to life" (Matthew 16:21).

When they got back to Galilee, He told them this again (Matthew 17:23). Then on the way to Jerusalem, He told them once more (Matthew 20:19). As Sir Norman Anderson says, "It seems incontrovertible that Christ Himself foretold His crucifixion and resurrection."

## He Died

Fundamental to any teaching on the resurrection is the need to establish that Jesus actually died. He didn't merely faint, as some Muslims teach, or merely appear to die. When Joseph of Arimathea asked Pilate for permission to bury the body of Jesus, "Pilate was surprised to hear that He was already dead. Summoning the centurion, he asked him if Jesus had already died" (Luke 15:44). The centurion confirmed that He had. There were several eye witnesses to His death.

It is highly improbable that anyone could survive crucifixion, especially if they had experienced violent flogging beforehand, as Jesus had. The body of Jesus was bandaged for the tomb and this process required the use of seventy-five pounds of ointment (John 19:39). If Jesus hadn't died on the cross, He certainly would have suffocated as His body was prepared for the grave.

# The Historical Reality of the Resurrection

Although no one actually witnessed the resurrection taking place, there were many who saw Jesus after the event. Some saw the place where His body had been laid with the folded but empty and, therefore, collapsed shroud still there. Others confirmed that they saw the Jesus they knew eating, walking and talking. On one occasion the risen Jesus was seen by a group of more than five hundred disciples.

Indeed, the appearance of the resurrected Jesus conquered the uncertainty and fear of one doubting disciple and turned the rest of the frightened, retiring group into a company of men who preached Jesus and His resurrection to the ends of the known world.

# If Jesus Didn't Rise From the Dead?

If the resurrection of Jesus didn't take place, then there is only one conclusion to be drawn: Christians are a deluded people who have misled millions of others for the past 2,000 years. Paul expresses this clearly when he says, "If Christ has not been raised, our preaching is useless and so is your faith. More than that, we are then found to be false witnesses about God" (1 Corinthians 15:14,15).

The argument of the New Testament is that Jesus did come back from the tomb and that He is therefore the prototype of a new man (1 Corinthians 15:20-23).

## The Problem of Sleep

One problem that arises here could be called the "problem of sleep." Death may seem to be the start of an exciting voyage to some, but to others it is clearly a false start.

They feel that before the ship reaches the harbor limit, it is whisked into a dry-dock and may have to wait a million years before the voyage can continue. They would say that after death we sleep until Christ comes, and at that point we actually go to enjoy heaven. Such a view is encouraged by our word *cemetery* which comes from the Greek word meaning "sleeping place."

When we turn to the New Testament, we certainly find that Paul makes some reference to "those who have fallen asleep" (1 Corinthians 15:20). One obvious reason for this would be Paul's Jewish background. The time before he became a Christian would have provided him with a view of survival after death that was closely akin to sleep. It is likely that he was simply making a statement about death that was so strongly colored with Old Testament thought that it had the effect of overriding any other picture within the word.

On the other hand, the New Testament speaks clearly of immediate resurrection after death. Jesus said to the penitent thief as they were both dying on their crosses, "Today you will be with Me in paradise" (Luke 23:43). To encourage us, the writer to the Hebrews tells us that we are "surrounded by such a great cloud of witnesses" (Hebrews 12:1).

We must acknowledge that there is a question about the meaning of "sleep" in the New Testament. Probably the answer has to do with time and eternity. It could be possible for two people to die millions of years apart and both immediately after death step into eternity at precisely the same moment. Eternity is not restricted by time.

The "problem of sleep" can never be completely resolved this side of heaven, but we can have confidence in the fact that the New Testament promises that when we make our *exodus* or departure from this world, we go straight to paradise.

# The Resurrection of the Believer

The Bible does not appear to predict a general resurrection of the dead, but teaches rather that there will be a definite moment in time when Jesus will come to take His Church to heaven. This will include all who have trusted in Him and who have died in the faith (1 Thessalonians 4:13-18). Jesus says that this group will "rise to live" (John 5:29) and enjoy "eternal life," having "crossed over from death to life" (John 5:24).

Then those outside Him will "rise to be condemned" (John 5:29) and "judged according to what they have done" (Revelation 20:12). The teaching of Scripture is that no one in the first group will be lost and no one in the second will be saved.

# An Answer to the Riddle of Life

Sigmund Freud wrote, "And finally there is the painful riddle of death, for which no remedy at all has yet been found, nor probably ever will be." According to Christian teaching, that is patently not true. The answer to the riddle of death is found in Christ. It is not a question of doing good things or believing the right teaching, but of having a living, personal faith in Jesus. He paid the penalty for our sins by His death on the cross, enabling us to be reconciled with God and to have eternal life.

If we believe in Him in this way, then at our burial or cremation our bodies will be sown into the ground as a "perishable" seed and will be "raised imperishable" (1 Corinthians 15:42); it will be "sown a natural body" and "raised a spiritual body" (1 Corinthians 15:44). It won't be the same body or even a reconstruction of the various parts, but it will be recognizable as *our* body. There will be continuity with the past, like a planted grain of wheat that eventually becomes a full grown stalk and ear.

## Being Eastered Ourselves

The New Testament writers not only speak about the resurrection of Jesus in the past tense but they also write of the resurrection of the believer in the past tense as well. What they appear to be stressing is that our future resurrection is so real and definite that there is a sense in which it has already taken place.

In his letter to the Christians in Ephesus, Paul uses three verbs translated into three English phrases to describe what has happened to the believer once he accepts Christ. He says God has "made us alive with Christ," "raised us up with Christ" and "seated us with Him in the heavenly realms."

John Stott says, "What excites our amazement, however, is that now Paul is not talking about Christ but *about us.* He is affirming not that God quickened, raised and seated Christ, but that He has quickened, raised and seated us with Christ."

The great distinctive characteristic of God's redeemed people pictured in Paul's letter to the Ephesians is not that they admire and worship Jesus, or live according to a new standard, or believe in a dynamically different way, but that, because of their being in Christ, they have actually begun to share in the ascension, resurrection and exaltation of Jesus.

John Stott continues:

Moreover, this talk about the solidarity with Christ in His resurrection and exaltation is not a piece of

meaningless Christian mysticism. It
bears witness to a living experience that
Christ has given us, on the one hand, a
new life (with a sensitive awareness of
the reality of God, and a love for Him
and for His people) and, on the other, a
new victory (with evil increasingly
under our feet). We were dead, but have
been made spiritually alive and alert.
We were in captivity, but have been
enthroned.

This, surely, is what Gerard Manley
Hopkins is referring to when he urges us
to let Christ "easter in us."

5

# Meditation
# Among
# the Tombs

# The Historical Event

There is a famous book titled *Meditation Among the Tombs* by Hervey. I have seen it in many second-hand book catalogs, although I have never actually handled a copy myself. Hervey's theme, the very end of people's lives, is neither morbid nor unusual. In older libraries you will probably find a whole shelf on this subject, including such volumes as Andrew Bonar's *The Last Day of Eminent Christians,* and *Death in Art and Epigram* by F. Parkes Webber.

Taking one of these books from the shelf and beginning to read is far from depressing. Indeed, even a hurried glance will reveal men and women who, on the threshold of death, were able to say with Mr. Despondency in *Pilgrim's*

*Progress,* "Farewell night, welcome day."
A German proverb says, "He that begins
to live begins to die." What these books
reveal is that some men and women
have discovered the secret of turning
death into life.

# Last Words

## Catherine Booth (1829-1890)

After her marriage to the founder of
the Salvation Army, William Booth,
Catherine spent a good deal of her time
seeking to improve the position of
women and children in society. She was
a gifted speaker in her own right. She
wasn't a strong child and in her last
years she suffered with cancer. Her last
words were:

> The waters are rising, but so am I.
> I'm not going under but over. Do not be
> concerned about dying; go on living
> well. The dying will be right.

## John Bunyan (1628-1688)

The tinker of Bedford, who gave the
world one of the great Christian classics,
*Pilgrim's Progress,* said as he died:

Weep not for me, but for your-
selves. I go to the Father of our Lord
Jesus Christ, who will, no doubt,
through the mediation of His eternal
Son, receive me, though a sinner; when
I hope we shall meet ere long to sing a
new song, and remain everlastingly
happy, world without end. Amen.

## William Carey (1761-1834)

The father of the modern missionary
movement was a shoemaker who so ap-
plied himself to study while repairing
shoes that by the time he was twenty he
could read the Bible in six languages. He
went on to spend more than forty-one
years on the mission field in India, and
was directly responsible for translating
portions of the Bible into thirty-six languages and dialects. His last words were:

When I am gone, say nothing about
Dr. Carey; speak about Dr. Carey's
Savior.

## John Wesley (1703-1791)

The founder of Methodism started
his working life as an assistant to his
father at the parish church in Epworth
before going as a missionary to Georgia

in the United States. He returned from there after three years, thoroughly discouraged and broken in health.

Through Moravians working in London, he experienced the full assurance of salvation on May 24, 1738. From that moment he became a traveling preacher, covering 250,000 miles, mainly on horseback, and preaching more than 40,000 sermons. He was a prolific writer, preacher and organizer.

He died in London after a short illness in 1791. He was almost eighty-eight years old. Twice in the last few moments of his life he cried out in triumph, "The best of all is, God is with us." His very last word was, "Farewell!"

## John Newton (1725-1807)

This gifted preacher and hymn writer is widely known as the author of *Amazing Grace*. Few lives, if any, reflect more amazing grace than his own. He changed from a hard-swearing sailor to a vicious West African slave trader, and then became a Christian, eventually becoming a leading evangelical in the Church of England and influencing such people as William Wilberforce and Hannah Moore. He died in his eighty-second year. His last words were:

> I am like a person going on a jour-
> ney in a stage coach, who expects its ar-
> rival every hour and is frequently
> looking out of the window for it . . . I am
> packed and sealed, and ready for the
> post.

## D. L. Moody (1837-1899)

D. L. Moody was the first evangelist of modern times whose preaching, along with the singing of Ira D. Stanley, led hundreds of thousands, if not millions, to Christ. His last words were: "I see earth receding; heaven is opening. God is calling me."

## Francis Schaeffer (1912-1984)

One of the foremost Christian apologists of the twentieth century, Francis Schaeffer started his working life as a part-time wet-fish salesman in America. He went on to popularize philosophy and establish the L'Abri study center in Switzerland.

While seriously ill with cancer, he managed a mammoth speaking tour linked with his last book, *The Great Evan-*

*gelical Disaster.* He died at home with his family in Rochester, Minnesota on May 15, 1984. They remembered him saying frequently during his last days, "His grace is sufficient."

## Martin Lloyd-James (1899-1981)

This gifted expositor and preacher followed Campbell Morgan as the minister of Westminster Chapel in London. Through his preaching, writing and his work among students, he was probably one of the greatest influences in the twentieth-century Christian church.

In February 1981, recognizing that his earthly task was finished, he said to his family, "Don't pray for healing," adding, "Don't try to hold me back from glory." He died peacefully in his sleep on March 1, 1981.

# Martyrs

The word *martyr* can easily conjure up images of a bygone age where heroic men and women in old-fashioned costumes are burned at the stake for their faith. Since Stephen, the first Christian martyr, laid down his life, many have been called to follow his example. If we take a closer look, the facts and figures of martyrdom are surprising. They suggest that the number of people who have died for their allegiance to Jesus Christ in the twentieth century is greater than the combined totals of every other century.

I thought about this a little while ago when I met Elisabeth Elliot. Her husband was martyred on January 8, 1956. Many people of my generation were moved by the deaths of Jim Elliot, Nate Saint, Pete Fleming, Ed McCully and Roger Youderian. These men were burdened to take the message of Jesus to the Auca Indians, a tribe living in the jungles of Ecuador who appeared to have had no contact with the outside world.

In a spirit true to the New Testament, Elisabeth Elliot took up the work for which her husband had laid down his life and went back with a tiny daughter to continue the work of trying to win the Aucas to the Christian faith. The fact that she was willing to do this probably accounted for the first Auca becoming a Christian.

Looking at martyrs in history is rather like looking at the deathbed

scenes earlier in this chapter. Rather
than being depressing, it is exhilarating
to see the faith and courage of these men
and women who, instead of playing safe,
were willing to chance death so that
others might believe.

Here is a handful of examples, just a
few of many stirring stories.

Jim Elliot (martyred January 8, 1956)

On Tuesday, January 3, 1956, Jim
Elliot and his four companions were up
at dawn, checking their equipment and
the small plane that was to fly them into
Auca territory. At 7 A.M. they had a time
of prayer and sang their favorite hymn,
"We Rest on Thee." On the last verse
their voices rang with deep conviction:

> We rest on Thee, our Shield and
>    our Defender,
> Thine is the battle, Thine shall be
>    the praise;
> When passing through the gates of
>    pearly splendor
> Victors, we rest with Thee through
>    endless days.

They had already spotted what they
thought would be a safe landing area on
a firm sandbar next to a river. They

called this "Palm Beach" and landed safely there, establishing their base camp.

On Friday, a group of Auca Indians arrived at the camp and were given trinkets, a machete and a model of the plane. A woman Auca, who the men called "Delilah," enjoyed looking at a copy of *Time*. They even took one of the Auca men for a flight over his own village.

Saturday was an anticlimax. The men waited with high hopes but not one of the Auca Indians appeared again.

At 4:30 A.M. on January 8, Nate's wife Marj switched on her radio to contact the men, expecting to hear that the Aucas had taken them to their village. There was no radio response from "Palm Beach." Just silence. They didn't know it at the time, but the men were already dead, killed by the lethal lances that all Auca men carried for both hunting and settling arguments.

The diaries of several of the men revealed that they had thought about the possibility of death and were even willing for this, if the Aucas could be won for Christ. Indeed, the pilot, Nate Saint, had broadcast on the missionary radio station HCJB:

God Himself laid down the law when He built the universe. He knew when He made it what the price was going to be. God didn't hold back His only Son, but gave Him up to pay the price for our failure and sin. Missionaries constantly face expendability. Jesus said, "There is no man that hath left house, or brethren, or sisters, or mother, or wife, or children, or lands for My sake and the Gospel's but shall not receive an hundredfold now in this time and in the world to come eternal life."

## Stephen (martyred A.D. 33)

With his willingness to serve, Stephen responded to the cry of help as men were needed to relieve the leaders of the early church of the more menial tasks, freeing them to concentrate on prayer and preaching (Acts 6:1-4). Acts 6 describes how the young church required spiritually qualified men to undertake the most practical and menial jobs.

It could have been Stephen's willingness to serve, as well as the fact that he was "full of the Spirit, wisdom, faith, grace and power" (Acts 6:3,5,8), that enabled him to move quickly to the place where he, too, was able to concentrate on preaching and teaching.

Very soon his public ministry was being opposed by the authorities in the synagogue, and they tried to silence him. He was arrested and made to appear before the Sanhedrin, the Jewish parliament. In reply to the charge of blasphemy, Stephen preached a sermon on God's dealings with His people since Abraham. In a bold and masterful way, he showed how it was the Jewish authorities who were wrong and not the young church.

The authorities "covered their ears and, yelling at the top of their voices, they all rushed at him, dragged him out of the city and began to stone him." Stephen "fell on his knees and cried out, 'Lord, do not hold this sin against them.' When he had said this, he fell asleep" (Acts 7:57,58,60).

## Polycarp (martyred February 23, A.D. 156)

Polycarp was the senior pastor of the church in Smyrna at the beginning of the second century. In A.D. 156, a sudden upsurge of persecution led by the Jews meant that eleven Christians were seized, tortured and thrown to wild animals. At the end of the orgy, the crowd clamored for the leader of the Christian church to be arrested and punished.

Polycarp was discovered on a farm outside the city, where he had refused to make any attempt to conceal his identity. He was arrested and, while food was set before his captors, he spent the time in prayer. The arresting party then set out for the stadium in Smyrna.

On their arrival, the vast crowd went wild. Somehow, above the noise, a voice rang out with the encouraging words, "Be strong, Polycarp, and play the man." The crowd demanded that Polycarp be thrown to the beasts. The proconsul tried to persuade him to swear an oath of allegiance to Caesar which would give him immediate freedom.

Polycarp refused with the memorable words, "For eighty-six years I have served Him, and He has never failed me. How can I revile my King and my Savior?"

On the grounds that the games were officially over, the proconsul refused the mob's request for Polycarp to be given to the animals. Instead, he ordered that he should die by fire. Such was the bitterness of the Jews toward Christians at the time that they broke their Sabbath commandment in hurrying to gather wood. Finally, Polycarp was tied to the stake and the fire lit, but the wind seemed to bend the flames around and above him. Polycarp prayed and a soldier used his sword to end the pastor's ordeal.

On February 23, A.D. 156, the Christian church in Smyrna knew what it meant to suffer for their faith. They also had a perfect example of the gentle spirit of witness and praise that could be theirs if they were called to walk the way of the martyr.

## Nicholas Ridley (martyred October 16, 1555)

Certainly in the ranks of the Reformers, no one deserves a higher place than Nicholas Ridley. Born in Northumberland near the Scottish border about 1500, he was educated at a local school in Newcastle upon Tyne and at Cambridge University. Upon graduation in 1524, he became a fellow of his college, Pembroke, and eventually its master in 1540. In the same year, he was appointed chaplain to Henry VIII. He became Bishop of London in 1550 and was nominated as the Bishop of Durham.

The death of the young King Edward VI halted Ridley's promotion in the Church of England. Indeed, Queen Mary so disliked his theology that he was an exception to her amnesty and was immediately confined to the Tower of London. He was taken from there to Oxford in 1554 to be insulted at a mock trial and finally burned at the stake with Hugh Latimer on October 16, 1555. The Martyrs Memorial in Oxford marks the site.

When the fire was lit at Ridley's feet, Hugh Latimer said, "Be of good comfort, Master Ridley, and play the man. We shall this day light such a candle, by God's grace in England, as I trust shall never be put out."

## Playing the Man

Christians down the ages have "played the man" while facing death in a variety of circumstances. Some have been martyred, many more ravaged by illness, others have faced the horrors of war, but most have been ordinary people coming to life's natural end. Simply to trace the facts of the few that we know about has been an inspiration to me. Perhaps the greatest pleasure has been to see the way that the evidence for Christ's resurrection has been underlined time and again.

C. S. Lewis put it so clearly:

Jesus has forced open a door that had been locked since the death of the first man. He has met, fought, and beaten the king of death. Everything is different because He has done so. This is the beginning of a new creation. The New Testament doesn't explain the resurrection of Jesus. But His resurrection certainly explains the New Testament.

## I Have Gone Home

On the slopes of a mountain in Kenya is a simple grave. The dean of Westminster Abbey had offered a place for the body of the Chief Scout, Lord Baden-Powell, between the graves of the Unknown Warrior and David Livingstone. But after consideration, the family declined the offer. With a guard of honor consisting of Boy Scouts from Africa, Europe and Asia, Lord Baden-Powell was buried instead in the Kenya he loved. The simple stone that marks the grave has on it a carved circle with a dot in the center—the Scout trail sign: "I have gone home."

For the believer, it couldn't be expressed more eloquently than that. The phrase also stands as a simple reminder that before we go home we need to get to know the Father and the family. Doing just that is the secret of "playing the man" both in life and in the face of death.

# Would You Like to Know God Personally?

# A Word From the Publisher

We hope you have enjoyed Ian Barclay's inspirational look at death and the life after. As he states so tellingly at the close, "Before we go home we need to get to know the Father and the family. Doing just that is the secret of 'playing the man' both in life and in the face of death."

The following four principles will help you discover how to know God personally and experience the abundant life He promised here on this earth and in the life after.

1. *God loves you, and created you to know Him personally.*

While the Bible is filled with assurances of God's love, perhaps the most telling verse is John 3:16:

> For God so loved the world, that He gave His only begotten Son, that whoever believes in Him should not perish, but have eternal life (NAS).

God not only loves each of us enough to give His only Son for us, He desires that we come to know Him personally:

> Now this is eternal life; that they may know you, the only true God, and Jesus Christ, whom you have sent (John 17:3).

What, then, prevents us from knowing God personally?

2. *Men and women are sinful and separated from God, so we cannot know Him personally or experience His love.*

We were all created to have fellowship with God; but, because of mankind's stubborn self-will, we chose to go our own independent way and fellowship with God was broken. This self-will, characterized by an attitude of active rebellion or passive indifference, is evidence of what the Bible calls sin.

For all have sinned and fall short of the glory of God (Romans 3:23, NAS).

The Bible also tells us that "the wages of sin is death" (Romans 6:23), or spiritual separation from God. When we are in this state, a great gulf separates us from God, because He cannot tolerate sin. People often try to bridge the gulf by doing good works or devoting themselves to religious or New Age practices, but the Bible clearly teaches that there is only one way to bridge this gulf . . .

3. *Jesus Christ is God's ONLY provision for our sin. Through Him alone we can know God personally and experience His love.*

God's Word records three important facts to verify this principle: (1) Jesus Christ died in our place; (2) He rose from the dead; and (3) He is our only way to God:

But God demonstrates His own love toward us, in that while we were yet sinners, Christ died for us (Romans 5:8, NAS).

Christ died for our sins . . . He was buried . . . He was raised on the third day according to the Scriptures . . . He appeared to Peter, then to the twelve. After that He appeared to more than five hundred (1 Corinthians 15:3-6, NAS).

Jesus said to him, "I am the way, and the truth, and the life; no one comes to the Father, but through Me" (John 14:6, NAS).

Thus, God has taken the loving initiative to bridge the gulf which separates us from Him by sending His Son, Jesus Christ, to die on the cross in our place to pay the penalty for our sin. But it is not enough just to know these truths . . .

4. *We must individually receive Jesus Christ as Savior and Lord; then we can know God personally and experience His love.*

John 1:12 records:

But as many as received Him, to
them He gave the right to become
children of God, even to those who
believe in His name (NAS).

What does it mean to "receive
Christ"? The Scriptures tell us that we
receive Christ through faith—not
through "good works" or religious en-
deavors:

For by grace you have been saved
through faith; and that not of your-
selves, it is the gift of God; not as a
result of works, that no one should
boast (Ephesians 2:8,9, NAS).

We're also told that receiving Christ
means to personally invite Him into our
lives:

(Christ is speaking): Behold, I
stand at the door and knock; if anyone
hears My voice and opens the door, I
will come in to him (Revelation 3:20,
NAS).

Thus, receiving Christ involves turning to God from self . . . and trusting
Christ to come into our lives to forgive
our sins and to make us the kind of
people He wants us to be.

# WOULD YOU LIKE TO KNOW GOD PERSONALLY?

If you are not sure whether you have
ever committed your life to Jesus Christ,
we encourage you to do so—today! Here
is a suggested prayer which has helped
millions of men and women around the
world express faith in Him and invite
Him into their lives:

*Lord Jesus, I want to know You per-
sonally. Thank You for dying on the cross
for my sins. I open the door of my life and
receive You as my Savior and Lord.
Thank You for forgiving my sins and
giving me eternal life. Take control of the
throne of my life. Make me the kind of person You want me to be.*

If this prayer expresses the desire of
your heart, why not pray it now? If you
mean it sincerely, Jesus Christ will come
into your life, just as He promised in
Revelation 3:20. He keeps His promises!
And there is another key promise to
write indelibly in your mind:

And the witness is this, that God
has given us eternal life, and this life is
in His Son. He who has the Son has the
life; he who does not have the Son of
God does not have the life. These things
I have written to you who believe in the
name of the Son of God, in order that

98

you may **know** that you have eternal
life (1 John 5:11-13, NAS).

That's right—the man or woman who
personally receives Christ as Savior and
Lord is assured of everlasting life with
Him in heaven. So, in summary, when
you received Christ by faith, as an act of
your will, many wonderful things happened, including the following:

1. Christ came into your life (Revelation 3:20 and Colossians 1:27).

2. Your sins were forgiven (Colossians 1:14).

3. You became a child of God (John
   1:12).

4. You received eternal life (John
   5:24).

5. You began the great adventure
   for which God created you (John
   10:10; 1 Thessalonians 5:18).

Thank you for considering this important message carefully. As you have
seen, what you do with it will determine
not only the quality of life you experience
now, but (most importantly) the quality
of life you will experience eternally.

If you have received Jesus Christ as your Savior and Lord, we heartily encourage you to attend and participate in a church where the Lord Jesus Christ is glorified, where the Holy Bible is honored and taught, and where believers love, encourage and pray for one another. Study God's Word regularly and apply it to your daily life. Share His love with your family, friends, co-workers and neighbors.

Perhaps a copy of this book would be of encouragement to someone you know. *Death and the Life After* is available in Christian bookstores, or from the publisher at 1-800-950-4457.

These four principles are adapted from *Would You Like to Know God Personally?* (Here's Life Publishers, 1987). Used by permission.

Finding Strength Within Grief

# ROSES IN DECEMBER

## by Marilyn Willett Heavilin

A mother who lost three sons offers sensitivity and comfort to others working through the grieving process. **Roses in December** will help you to deal with your loss, understand your grief, and find your own roses in the dark days of your life.

> *"One of the best books I've read for those who have lost a loved one."*
> —Florence Littauer

## At Christian bookstores everywhere.

Or call